Peak Performance Interviewing for Executives

The Insider's Strategy for Winning Job Interview Success for C-Suite Positions

MORITA METHOD ©
ACADEMY

RAINER MORITA

International Job Search Coach
Hidden Job Market Advisor
Executive Resume Writer
Website: www.Morita-Academy.com

To all executives

who know their unique value and
want to win in interviews,

TABLE OF CONTENTS

ABOUT THE AUTHOR

Rainer Morita is the founder of the Morita Academy that helps executives become authentic and highly effective leaders. As an International Job Search Coach and Hidden Job Market Expert he coaches executives how to find their perfect job based on the Morita Method. He authored three books: *"Executive Job Search in the Hidden Job Market - The Morita Method"*, *"Tokyo Expat Job Search Guide"* and *"Find Your Passion."* He has coached more than 5,000 top-tier executives worldwide and has more than 17 years' experience in Executive Search. He regularly prepares IMD (Lausanne and Singapore) and INSEAD (Paris, Abu Dhabi and Singapore) alumni for interviews and holds job search seminars for an international audience at the Tokyo Institute of Technology, Technical University, Dresden, RWTH Aachen University International Academy, Germany, in cooperation with Maastricht School of Management in the Netherlands, as well as Al Akhawain University in Morocco. You can contact him at contact@moritamethod.com.

FOREWORD

After interviewing more than 5000 executives, during the last 17 years in executive search and advisory roles, I realized that they needed a better approach to interviewing.

Despite thousands of career and job search guides, dedicated books on how-to interview, and the advice of many career and job search experts, most executives continue to fail in interviews because of a serious performance gap.

In my search for a better solution, I distilled, tested, and optimized my interview experiences with all kinds of executives worldwide into a simple methodology allowing dramatic performance improvements in the shortest period of time to win interviews.

My relentless pursuit of excellence and total commitment to helping anyone become the number one candidate for the hiring manager, led to the term "Peak Performance Interviewing" or simply PPI.

It is my fondest hope that "Peak Performance Interviewing" will help you win interviews so that you get the job you deserve and love.

PEAK PERFORMANCE INTERVIEWING FOR EXECUTIVES

*"The biggest room in the world is
the room for improvement."*

— Japanese proverb

HISTORY – THE ORIGIN OF PPI

First, let's take a quick look at the origin of Peak Performance Interviewing (PPI). In my role as an executive search consultant, I have interviewed more than 5000 international executives at all levels, across all corporate functions, and various industries. I have successfully contributed to the placement of more than 100 candidates over the last 17 years. Being an executive search consultant, my Key Performance Indicator was clear. Help candidates be the number one in the job search game and get hired. Number two and number three don't count. All that matters is being number one. The obvious question that comes to mind is why? Well, number two and number three never get the job, and as a result, I don't get paid either. Therefore, I had to unrelentingly focus on only one thing: Making my candidate win the first position among all other candidates.

"Unlike the Olympics, in the job hunting game, there is no such thing as a silver medal for number two or bronze medal for number three. There is only one winner and the rest are all losers."

- Rainer Morita

WHY PPI? GET HIRED

The goal of PPI is to be number one in interviews and land the job you love.

How does PPI work? Two PPI Principles

The two principles of PPI are focus and simplicity.

Brutal Focus on Value

The principle of focus means you must radically focus on value. If you go through different rounds of interviews with different interviewers, focus on each specific interviewer's value perception at a time. Focus here means that you create maximum value for the interviewer to solve his/her main growth problem, or issue, for which he is seeking you.

Radical Simplicity

The principle of simplicity means that you must make things as simple as possible.

Albert Einstein was a great friend of simplicity. His general recommendation was

> *"Everything should be as simple as possible, but not simpler."*
> - Albert Einstein

Simplicity has value. That is what companies and employees value in tomorrow's leaders and expect from you in interviews.

> *"Great leaders are almost always great simplifiers, who can cut through argument, debate, and doubt to offer a solution everybody can understand."*
> ~Colin Powell~

Easy to understand = true

People tend to believe things that are easy to understand. Psychologists call this cognitive fluency. Contrary-wise, they believe less in things that are hard to understand. Using simplicity is therefore in your best interest, because you can more easily win over the interviewer to your opinion: Hiring you is best for him.

People tend to make the simple complicated. The interview scenario favors simplicity. Make the complicated awesomely simple. So simple that a six-year old can understand you. Or, your grandmother who often is not familiar with your industry, or that of your favorite employer.

> **PPI helps you to radically focus on what matters most and deliver it in the simplest way – VALUE.**

HOW DOES PPI WORK? THE THREE INTERVIEWING TECHNIQUES OF PPI

PPI employs three of the following interviewing techniques, which I developed on my own and decided to label them as follows:

1) Rapid Prototyping

2) Meat over the bone

3) Closing the deal

RAPID PROTOTYPING – THE FIRST PPI INTERVIEWING TECHNIQUE

I took the idea of Rapid Prototyping from my master dissertation thesis and applied it to interviewing. First, what is Rapid Prototyping? The basic idea is to rapidly conduct a series of prototyping cycles with the aim to continuously improve the prototype before making a final product. In other words, quickly debug and optimize the prototype in many small steps to achieve a major improvement, possibly a breakthrough. The logic behind that for companies is that hundreds if not thousands of Rapid Prototypes produce a much better result than the first trial quick shot. Now, what is the connection with interviewing? I want you to Rapid Prototype your interview core messages. Before I continue, let me share with you a secret to overcoming a much neglected interview problem.

I got so nervous and didn't know what to do.

We all know, from interviews, that suddenly we get nervous. You talk with a strange voice. You are staggering, your lips and fingers are shivering. Some people even encounter complete blackout, with the loss of what to say or are unable to say what they prepared themselves to say. The old, too common, problem all of us encounter is that things no longer work as we expected them to work. You find your best messages, ideas, lines of thought and reasoning, tactics and prepared answers, difficult to find or remember. Many people consider this is normal, but it derails all your interview preparation and lowers your interview score. What a shame! Is there nothing that can be done about it?

The world on the wrong track

Most advice on interviewing is ineffective. There are more than 6000 books on interviewing and thousands of coaches, counselors, and trainers who try to help jobseekers regarding interviewing around the globe. However, these are in vain. Despite the best advice and coaching available, people continue to mess up in interviews. But why?

Using sentences and paragraphs do not work

Most career and job search coaches, counselors and trainers, have their job seeking clients practice with long sentences, or even paragraph with several sentences. On Amazon, I could find more than 5000 hits with the keywords "interview questions". Most of those career experts give readers the illusion of perfect answers. Books are filled with interview questions and ideal answers. The problem is, those answers tend to be long. Long sentences, one after another. The job seekers are made to believe that learning those long answers is a good way to prepare for interviews. Some job seekers even memorize answers believing that this is the ultimate effort and best preparation.

Unfortunately, this does not work.

For one, great companies in search of exceptional talent ask smart atypical questions. Google, for example, has such interviewing intelligence built into their process that renders scripting and memorizing ineffective.

For another, there is a magic force that renders our learning efforts futile. What is this magic force?

THE DESTRUCTIVE NATURE OF ADRENALINE

The magic force is adrenaline. Adrenaline messes up our normal brain functioning and normal demeanor. Why is that?

Adrenaline is a survival hormone. The moment we face the interviewer, we secrete a massive amount of adrenaline that puts us in survival mode. We feel as if we are facing a threat to our lives such as when facing a scorpion, python, shark or gorilla. Survival mode means that adrenaline sabotages the brain from properly working so that we can run away. Although you want to behave naturally at the interview and ignore anything that makes you nervous, you cannot suppress the body's fight for survival. In your fight for survival, you are unable to remember simple things, let alone long sentences; you cannot reason logically, or appear calm, relaxed and assertive. Most of the time, but not always, your body language is also speaking the language of the fight for survival, although that is exactly the opposite of what you want.

For example, most executives that I rehearse interviews with even forget stating their own name, their company name and their title when introducing themselves. This is adrenaline. You see how destructive adrenaline can be?

Now you realize how futile it is to try remembering to speak long sentences when facing an alligator's open mouth full of sharp teeth. It simply doesn't work. Therefore, it is ineffective to follow the interview question-and-answer model with an attempt to build interviewing power from emulating so called "perfect answers." For one, your brain will not do you this favor because of the destructive nature of adrenaline. In addition, perfect answers are anything but perfect because they do not exactly fit your case. Finally, nobody likes candidates who sound like a tape recorder, mechanical, robot-like and fake. That's not being authentic.

In conclusion, most career books and advice giving you a list of questions and long answers lead you on the wrong path and to mediocre interview outcomes. So, what's a better way of dealing with the unavoidable adrenaline problem?

USE KEYWORDS ONLY

Use the minimum number of Keywords, and Keywords only. This is because Keywords are something you can remember despite adrenaline. Let me give you an example from a different scenario.

What do politicians, celebrities, and big shot executives often do before or during their keynote speeches? What do famous TV show moderators often do, in order to deliver an unmatched presentation? What do a lot of masters of ceremony do in order to deliver a masterful event experience? They use Keywords. Written on the backside of blank index cards. Keywords help them to deliver a powerful speech, run an awesome show, or moderate an event in the best possible way.

Finding the Right Keywords

The search for the right Keywords is a search for maximum value. Ask yourself: What provides maximum value for the interviewer? What would solve the number one growth problem of the interviewer?

There are various techniques for generating Keywords. Brainstorming, talking with peers, recruiters, mentors, job search coaches, management consultants, stock analysts, journalists, executives and alumni of the company you interview with, etc.

In some cases, you might also search for various job descriptions which all are close to your target job. You'll find a lot of job specs on the internet, both on job portals or on the homepage of the hiring company or its competitors. You highlight important words in the job spec and then select the most important ones. They could become your Keywords.

MEAT OVER THE BONE – THE SECOND PPI INTERVIEWING TECHNIQUE

In the absence of information, people assume the worst. Interviewers doubt you. That means they will do some deeper probing to get the information you withhold from them. It also means that your interview performance suffers because your messages are incomplete and therefore of less impact.

This problem relates most to accomplishments.

The idea behind meat over the bone originated in the poor quality of accomplishments. Crisply defined well-presented accomplishments mean high punching power in interviews. That determines your competitiveness in interviews. Meat over the bone makes sure you obtain maximum punching power by optimizing your accomplishment story.

The use of the words "meat over the bone" comes from looking at resumes. Most resumes I get have a long list of poorly formulated accomplishments, sometimes 10 to 15 listed with bullet points. There is so little information about what was accomplished, that is why I call that superficial way of calling your accomplishments "bones" and the missing contextual information "meat over the bones". When you glance at poor resumes, they look like a skeleton. You only see the bones. No WOW-factor anywhere, or not enough of it. A good resume with attractive accomplishments, however, is like meat over the bone.

In PPI, Meat over the bone applies to any statement you make, in particular accomplishments. Statements with Meat Over the Bone have substance; they have evidence and are therefore credible – and therefore they are good. The more good messages you make, the better the interview. It's that simple. Whether you talk about your strengths, core competencies, learning curve, performance, ability to execute or handle ambiguity in international settings: provide evidence in the form of quantitative or qualitative descriptions.

CLOSING THE DEAL – THE THIRD INTERVIEWING TECHNIQUE IN PPI

Closing the deal is from the world of advertising campaigns. How do TV commercials usually finish? A TV commercial for a car, for example, although it could be any product, how does it finish? Almost all finish with a call to action or punch-line. Telling people what to do … Dial a number to make appointment with a car dealer or visit a website. Why is that? To move people to action at the end of which they should decide to buy a car. This is what I mean by "Closing the Deal". Tell people to take action. From moving to the next interview round, to moving the hiring process forward to verbal and paper offers, and, ultimately, hiring you.

What about commercials without a call for action? Most are ineffective and go up in smoke. That is why it is so important to close the deal in the interview.

> **Tell the interviewer to hire you.**

Tell people to hire you. Otherwise, you risk beating around the bush. Let me explain. Two busy executives, you and the interviewer, convene, not rarely after traveling a considerable distance and preparing for the meeting with the purpose of hiring you or not hiring you. As the word job interview says, you interview for a job, for employment. Amazing as it may seem, most interviews conclude without conclusions. Neither the interviewer, nor the interviewee touches the question: Why don't you just hire me?

Overcoming Hiring Procrastination: Hire me!

> **Ask to be hired. Repeat it many times.**

At the executive hiring level, procrastination of the hiring manager for making the hiring decision is one of your greatest obstacles you must overcome to get the job. Paradoxically, the person who most needs you struggles with making a decision that would solve his problem. The reason for that is hiring managers are risk-adverse and hiring someone external is a big risk. Therefore, statistics show that in about 40% of all hirings, procrastination sabotages hiring. This maybe due to an age bias, industry bias, perfect candidate illusion, paralysis by analysis, budget concerns, delaying the hiring process endlessly, etc.

To overcome procrastination and make more impact, I recommend interviewees to ask the interviewer for the job. How?

HIRE ME!

Make a command. "Hire me!"

Do not make a request. Do not ask a question. In both cases you lose power by ceding control.

The best and most effective way is to tell him what to do in the shortest and punchiest way: "Hire me!". Hiring you is imperative. There is no other choice. If the interviewer really wants the value you project, you are the solution. Period.

> **Liberate yourself from the wrong belief
> that asking for the job is taboo**

The feedback I receive from my clients about "Hire me!" is in most cases staggeringly positive. Liberating. They get rid of the old belief that asking for the job is a taboo and adopt the new belief that "Hire me!" makes so much sense to ask and makes their interview so much more effective.

This may be tough for leaders with a background in engineering or science who tend to be humbler than their colleagues in sales. Especially for this tendency it will make you stand out among similar candidates and create a high impact on the interviewer. Rehearse and apply it in your next interview.

Do not use if sentences such as "If there is an opening, then…" or "If you need somebody like me, then …" because you are talking possibilities and giving him choices. Saying no or simply not doing anything is a convenient option. You see that possibility thinking is not effective for breaking the interviewer's hiring procrastination during the short period of time of an interview.

Hire me! Is a wake up call and emotional handshake. It is an electric jolt that goes deep into the interviewer's gut, not his brain. This is good because most hiring decisions are based on emotions and justified with facts.

Essentially, if you don't ask or tell anything, you are unlikely to get anything. Like in a restaurant, if you don't place an order, you don't get anything to eat.

"But this does not work in our culture."

I hear this objection many times. I acknowledge many objections to the "Hire me!" approach saying that it will not work in the cultural context of the country where the interview takes place. "This is one of those new ideas, but I can't say such a thing there." I get those objections from candidates in Germany, Switzerland, Singapore, China, Japan, etc. just to name a few.

Value-based hiring works anywhere worldwide, yet, there are a few countries you need to watch out for. In countries and cultures where some interviewers tend to value relationships more than value, such as Japan or some Arab countries, you may have to place emphasis on relationships first and value second. But even Japan, with the breaking apart of big corporate networks and the rise of performance-based pay systems, value is becoming more and more important. And even conservative Saudi-Arabia, which is privatizing big government-owned companies and is eager about job creation in private industry, will not be able to neglect the importance of value in hiring for long.

Value-based interviewing, such as PPI, allows you to breakthrough cultural barriers. Value is universally applicable and universally attractive. Hiring managers find candidates attractive who bring in much more than what they cost. Hire me! … is based on value works.

How you communicate is as important as what you communicate.

Important, however, is how you communicate your message.

Note that "Hire me!" must come across firm and natural without the shadow of a doubt on your lips. As natural as making an order in a restaurant. If you provide superior value for the interviewer and hiring manager, your "Hire me!" must come across as a no-brainer. As natural as ripe apple falling from the tree. The value you offer is so strong that is makes thinking superfluous.

Let's for a moment look at how companies decide about buying external professional services. Let us assume the company is in negotiations with an advertising agency for commissioning an entire marketing campaign. The agency shows a 10 times return on the required investment where the company would recover the initial investment after a short time. No risk. Let us also assume that all other factors of hiring an agency has been completely addressed. The decision maker is therefore standing to win hugely from this deal and is made to believe "I would be stupid not to hire this agency." This is exactly what you need to achieve in interviewing.

> **Lead the interviewer's thinking. Lead him to believe, and ultimately draw the conclusion, that you are the best candidate he must hire to succeed.**

Note that I am not advocating the ice-breaker approach of standing up and shouting "Hire me!" but rather the _tipping point approach_. This is not so much about breaking ice but rather like moving the interviewer's perception over the tipping point where hiring you appears as HIS/HER only possible correct choice.

Repeat "Hire me!"

It is essential is to repeat it many times. Once or twice is not enough. Maybe three to five times, depending on the interview scenario. As always, use it in context. Use it wisely. Parroting will backfire on you.

Repetition is a simple, yet powerful technique to persuade. You see the same ads for brands many times. Politicians repeat the same messages again and again. This is especially true during election campaigns. Journalists repeatedly express the same opinion. Repetition is indeed one of the easiest and most widespread techniques to persuade people. Therefore, to increase the impact of "Hire me!" on the interviewer, use it several times.

You are better because you offer more value. It's as simple as that. For that reason, repeat your message until the hiring managers arrives at the conclusion that hiring you is indeed the best solution for the company.

How can I soften "Hire me", if I must soften my style?

Some scenarios require you to soften your messages. Especially female candidates need to avoid strong statements when strong personalities are not what the interviewer is looking for.

For example: if the interviewer values soft style for his corporate culture, if in certain cases, some interviewers value submissive candidates. I had a strong-willed second generation owner and CEO from an Indian pharmaceutical company strongly prefer a submissive Indian female Global HR Director. Many Japanese and Arab companies value submissive female candidates because it is so deeply entrenched in Japanese and Arab society and culture.

Similar cases may be a conservative Swiss firm with strong preferences for candidates from certain "Cantons" (which is Swiss word for prefecture) or a traditional Japanese who values a seniority system or an Indian aristocrat who is sky high in the Indian cast system. What should you do in those cases?

One approach is to use "Hire me!" followed by a softener such as "What is the next step?"

Another approach is dropping "Hire me" entirely and asking the question "Do you have any concerns that would keep you from recommending me for this job?"

THE PPI PREP

The three most important interview questions in the PPI Prep are as follows:

> **Number one: Tell me something about yourself.**
>
> **Number two: What are you good at?**
>
> **Number three: What can you do for us?**

PPI Prep stands for Peak Performance Interview Preparation. I choose "prep" because executives looking for a job must prepare for several interviews, sometimes even an interview marathon. In cross-border and maybe cross continent searches 20 to 25 interviews all with different companies are not rare. You realize the importance of things for preparation must go quickly. Especially executives searching during their tenure are time conscious.

PPI is designed as a quick pull-out-of-your-sleeves-and-put-back-into-your-pockets method. And the reason is obvious. With maximum focus and upmost simplicity, we can achieve solid interview preparation in the least amount of time possible.

Question 1) Tell me something about yourself

This invitation is a blunter version of the same question: Who are you? This is a tricky question, much trickier than you think because it is not so much a question of introducing yourself.

Let me explain what the interviewer really wants to know. First and foremost, the interviewer is obsessed with whether you are bringing the right value. In other words, "Does this interviewee offer the value I am looking for?"That is his primary concern, and much less who the person is.

Therefore, you must first tell the interviewer why they should hire you. The reason for hiring you is your value. Tell him your unique value. Now you understand why the old school way of introducing yourself starting with college, degree, first job until last job would earn you minus points, because at this critical stage of opening the interview you're waffling about 20 or 30 years with no relevance to value creation. This makes it boring in the interviewer's perspective, priorities, and interest.

Only after telling him your value does the interviewer get curious about who you are. Since you addressed well his burning desire for value, you need to explain at the next stage about yourself. VALUE first, YOU and YOUR BACKGROUND second.

Old school interviewing is a full-blown self-introduction. Value-based interviewing will give him a mini-bio which is extremely short and only focuses on that part of your experience that explains what relates to the value you offer, which is the reason for hiring you. Don't be surprised. A snippet of one or two sentences will suffice.

Finally, you need to answer his implicit question "Why are you interviewing here today if you are able to offer such fantastic value?" Tell him why you are job searching and why you are interested in working for the interviewer or his organization.

To recapitulate, the first question "Who are you?" comprises three questions:

Who are you? Why should we hire you? And, why are you interested in our company? But, you need to start your answer by explaining why we should hire you.

Question 2): What are you good at?

This question is about telling your strengths. Select one. Only one. The one that helps you create the extraordinary value you are promising the interviewer. This, and nothing more, would be spot on.

Let us look at a case of General Electric interviewing for a global sales director of a company that they recently acquired.

Most interviewees gave the interviewer the following answers:

*   I am excellent at business development and able to create new business.
*   I am outstanding global business developer able to access new markets or penetrate existing ones.
*   I am good at creating new alliances to pool resources and sell more in a joint effort.
*   I am good at buying other companies to grow the company faster than anybody else in the company's history.
*   I am an excellent strategist able to improve performance with a superior marketing and business strategy.

All these answers are pointing at increasing revenue. Most of you would agree that all answers above make sense for a global sales director position.

But, the main challenge of the company was integration with General Electric after the acquisition. Therefore, the right answer is: I am good at teamwork. In the leadership language of General Electric, the perfect word is "inclusion." General Electric was looking for someone who understood the "GE Way" and the people and culture of this European niche technology leader and help to integrate the acquired company into the GE network of companies.

Question 3) What can you do for us?

THE one question that matters most in interviews/

THE most important interview questions in PPI is,

WHAT CAN YOU DO FOR US?

Why? This is THE question that focuses on value. I call it the value question. It focuses on what value you can create for the hiring manager. The candidate who offers most value by solving the hiring manager's growth challenge, in the best possible way, and convincingly communicates so, wins the interview. Executives must not only propose superior value but also show execution capability. This is especially true for Private Equity, an industry that is built on the idea of added value.

For a CEO, it means showing how you plan to execute your business plan or showing how you plan to execute the business plan of the hiring organization. For a functional head, it means how you can help the CEO execute the business plan and achieve his or her goals.

The answer to "What can you do for us?" is about your Unique Value Proposition. Make sure your Unique Value Proposition is irresistible. Also, make sure you have a plan on how to execute your Unique Value Proposition.

It is good to know that you must focus your time, preparation and delivery of your message on one single question. It boosts your confidence as I can attest from hundreds of interview preparation cases. Take the opposite case. Books suggesting 49, 200 or even 500 of the toughest interview questions are misleading and confusing. People get lost. What is most important will remain guesswork.

Merits of PPI for Your Job Search

- Learn in 60 minutes the most essential skill for turning interviews into successful outcomes and job offers: Demonstrate how you can deliver value.

- PPI is a simple logical framework that helps to keep things short and simple.

- PPI triggers a shift in your behavior from passive easy to intimidate and rather anxious job applicant towards a proactive interviewee who talks and acts with confidence and entrepreneurial attitude from the eyes of the interviewer, his/her advisor or the interest of the hiring organization as a whole.

- Knowing why interviewers ask certain questions and what is the story behind them.

- Good framework to train with a sparring partner before interviews. PPI helps to become more focused and to get into Peak Performance Interviewing shape.

- PPI makes you confident because you know your value and how to communicate it effectively in a simple way.

- PPI gets you to the heart of the matter and enables you to find out fast what is going on in the interviewer's mind and how he is thinking about hiring you. Closing the deal and do it repeatedly.

- PPI allows you to be more present and engaged with the interviewer with authentic, natural and fresh answers.

- Transforming an interview into a baby chat. When you apply the three PPI techniques correctly, interviewing becomes like a baby chat. This is what you want. If you communicate so well that a six-year old or even a baby understands you, you are top of the game. You will – whether you like it or not – benefit from this baby chat communication style. That's what makes PPI so powerful. If you are able to take out the complexity and heaviness of an interview conversation and transform it into a baby chat between two equals, you are there. You are authentic, effective, easy to understand, engaging and likeable. What else could you wish for?

THE ILLUSION OF THE PERFECT CANDIDATE

> **PERFECT CANDIDATES DO NOT EXIST. ONLY GOOD MATCHES, AND GOOD INTERVIEWING PERFORMANCE.**

Perfect candidates do not exist. Only good matches, and good interviewing performance.

Especially after reading poor job specifications which are a list of nearly impossible nice-to-have items for the employer (but tell nothing about what successful job performance looks like) candidates often feel discouraged. "I have no chance. That's impossible for me to make it," and similar thoughts occupy their minds. Even statements like "I will give it a try Rainer, but I feel I am miles away from what they want." This is mind pollution and sabotages your best efforts for peak performance. Unless you have a winner's attitude, how can you convince the interviewer that you are a winning candidate for them.

Don't let the illusion of the perfect candidate catch you. In the end it is only an illusion.

In other words, I give up the illusion that the best candidate is the one who satisfies all decision-makers' requirements perfectly, at a 100 percent.

Instead, the best candidate is the one who is lacking a good portion of what the decision-makers are looking for, and yet, convincingly presents himself as the best available candidate in the market.

A lot of executive search agents agree on this point that the near-to-perfect candidate is undesirable. A lot of those candidates get easily bored because they are all too familiar with the job assignment and sooner or later they decide to quit.

From a career development perspective, your career move should bring a fresh set of skills that enrich your career skill portfolio. Therefore, it is also in your own interest to interview for a role that is too big for you and offers potential for growth.

Depending on the scenario, candidates with a 60 to 80% match with hiring specifications are a much healthier and better choice for both the candidate and the hiring manager.

Candidates with 20 to 40% of lacking skills as measured against the official hiring specification, are often more desirable and more valuable than the perfect match.

When coaching first-time CEO contenders, they are frequently struggling with articulating their value because in their mind they are desperately searching for the CEO experience that the job spec is asking for, but they are lacking. Any CEO aspiring the ascent to power as CEO simply needs to accept that any first time CEO contender does not have prior CEO experience and that this is fine. The total combination of experience.

Yet, some things are easier said than done. Despite me explaining this to you now, this long-held belief takes some people longer to accept than expected. When preparing people for interviews, I notice them falling back into deficiency-thinking caused by the perfect-candidate illusion. I also notice a significant rise in their level of confidence after reassuring them that they still have a good chance to win.

Peak Performance to Turn the Odds In Your Favor

If you are one of those far-from-the-perfect-matches, less-than-the-ideal candidate-type- with-limits-or-no-industry-experience type of executive interviewee, you realize that you may not have a real chance at any interview. In that case, deliver peak performance in interviews and position yourself strongly to win. I am not saying here that industry experience is not important for interviews or that any company with stringent hiring standards including industry experience will hire you. No that is not the message.

Thousands of top executives get hired every month against all odds. And, it will be like that next month and next year as well.

> **Focus on the few companies where you have a real chance to win and ignore the clear majority of others which will reject you. Then strike hard with PPI and win interviews.**

Let me repeat it, because it is so difficult for executives to internalize this despite mainstream media and recruiter wisdom tells them daily:

Seemingly weak candidates can move mountains with PPI. If this is you, yes, you too, can get hired with strong interview performance where your value is king.

> **Don't be blinded and discouraged by most companies disliking and rejecting you for valid or far-fetched reasons, but be 10000 times focused on the vital few companies where you can play a big and winnable game worth playing. Use PPI to win interviews and land offers**

Let me highlight for you several cases where candidates got hired against all expectations.

Case 1 – Tesla Motors - VP of Asia – Robin Ren

For Tesla Motors the Chinese market was and is most important after the US. Therefore, the hire of its Head of Asia was key to assure market success in China and key Asian markets. In May 2016, Tesla Motors did not hire one of the many automotive executives from the Chinese market but an IT executive from the Bay Area. More precisely speaking, the new VP of Asia at Tesla Motors was and still is Robin Ren who joined Tesla after an IT career in California. He held positions of increasing responsibility at Yahoo, Senior Engineering Manager, Dell, Director of Software Engineering, VMWare, Director R&D, Cloud Applications and Services, CTO of EMC and finally BU Director of XtremeIO with EMC leading it to the fastest-to-$1B IT product ever.

Case 2 – Deutsche Bank – Global CIO Hire – Kim Hammonds

In 2016, Deutsche Bank faced huge debts, billions of dollars in lawsuit liabilities and was struggling with old, costly, ineffective IT systems, causing, among other things, low productivity. Lowering inflated IT related costs while modernizing the entire IT system to raise productivity was the mission of a new CIO to be hired. Deutsche Bank could have found many internal or external candidates speaking English and German with rock-solid IT banking experience. In this crisis situation, Deutsche Bank appointed a mid-forty-year old Kim Hammonds from California, who neither had experience in banking nor inside the financial service industry at large. She was from Boeing, in the USA, where she spent most her career and she did not speak any German. After a short period as CIO she advanced to the role of Group COO.

Case 3 – Nestle Global CEO Hire – Ulf Mark Schneider

The Swiss company, Nestle, is the world's largest food and beverage company with about 335,000 employees. In 2016, Nestle's Chairman, Mr. Barbeck, appointed a new CEO. There was only one external candidate competing with a series of strong internal candidates including the Head of its Asia, Oceania and Africa Region, Wan Lin Martello who also served as previous Group CFO; Head of Business Excellence, Chris Johnson and Head of the Americas, Laurent Freixe. To the surprise of all, the external candidate, Ulf Mark Schneider, got the job although he was hardly known in Switzerland and did not even have a food and beverage background. And he got a stellar compensation package of 14 million Swiss Francs per year.

Case 4 – Kraft Heinz CFO Appointment – 29-year old David Knopf

Since the mega Kraft Heinz merger in 2015, the company has not been able to grow revenue. The company became known for cost-cutting rather than introducing new brands. Share prices fell 6.5% in 2017. In 2017, David Knopf made it to the C-Suite of this USD100BN American Fortune 500 company at the age of 29, which made him the company's youngest CFO ever and among one of the youngest CFOs of a major US corporation. The Kraft Heinz leadership shakeup and the David Knopf CFO appointment were an attempt to revive the company's sluggish sales.

Case 5 – Jenoptik GmbH CEO Appointment – Lothar Spaeth

Jenoptik company (ex VEB Zeiss Jena), was one of the few former Eastern German state-owned enterprises, which survived the transformation into a market economy in a united Germany. It was one of the few East German firms that was thought to have a realistic chance of competing in a global market. From 1991 to 2003, he headed Jenoptik and played a pivotal role in the transformation from state-owned to globally competitive private enterprise. Lothar Spaeth was a German politician and Minister President of Baden-Wuerttenberg (which is a German federal state or "Bundesland" as it is called in German and an industrial powerhouse in Germany) from 1978 to 1991.

You may object: "But, this is not me. I am not so famous, not such a high ranked executive, not so high potential."

Let me assure you. You are, but you are refusing to see the truth: All great leaders start out as ordinary people.

The above list of cases could go on and on. And you will also find them in your industry, at your level of seniority and compensation and in your age group. More often than you think Fortune 500 and other executives join professional service firms as partners; professional service firm executives – as for example those from advertising agencies, consultancies, auditing firms, just to name a few – become C-Suite executives for leading private firms; and senior government officials join private industry in leadership roles. Yearly, thousands of executives win interviews and secure (mostly hidden) jobs – despite all odds. To learn more of how you, too, can secure yourself those hidden executive jobs, read *"Executive Job Search in the Hidden Job Market - The Morita Method"* (www.moritamethod.com)

PPI GENERATES AUTHENTIC LEADERS

PPI generates Authentic Leaders. I call such executives authentic leaders because they showcase not only their strong side, but also have the guts to admit their weaknesses. This is natural and also more credible. For example, shallow experience, lack of certain client connections, lack off big corporate experience, not speaking the language of headquarter executives, having more B2B vs. B2C background, and so on and so forth.

PPI means telling the naked truth about yourself, means telling a true story, and also coming across as a trustworthy, congruent leader. You are the authentic leader.

ACTION LEARNING

According to Confucius, *I hear, and I forget; I see, and I remember; I do, and I understand.*

PPI is Action Learning. Action learning is an approach to solving real problems that involve taking action and reflecting upon the results. The learning that results helps improve the problem-solving process as well as the solutions the team develops.

PPI is about what you say, not what you think, neither what you think you will say.

> **If you cannot say your message in the way that a six-year-old or your grandmother will understand, you must practice interviewing.**

THE IMPORTANCE OF A SPARRING PARTNER

To reach maximum potential in interviewing, you need a sparring partner. In boxing, professional boxers use sparring partners to train and prepare for important fights. The reason is that two people are necessary for boxing. The best and only real practice is the two-person combat. Boxing sacks, hopping cords, weight-lifting, running, etc. are all substituted for this essential boxing training.

Boxing is a dynamic combat, and you need practice with a real person. You learn from his actions, tactics, strategies, clues, and many other things. You learn only in combating that person what to do, and you also learn what not to do. Especially in boxing, a mistake in a second can lead to a knock-out and your loss.

Now, you recognize how valuable a sparring partner can be for a two-person combat such as interviewing. Let me recapitulate that the sparring partner is the purest form of Action Learning for interviewing. You would pay the highest tribute to Confucius who said that practice is the only way to master a task.

Think about it for a moment:

- How can you factor in the personality of an interviewer you have never met?

- How can you factor in unusual questions from the interviewer that has probing, provoking or stress-testing purposes?

- How can you factor in emotional issues such as humor, wit, irony, embarrassment on the side of the interviewer?

- How can you factor in the influence of several interviewers at the same time?

More important questions are:

- How do you know how you perform?

- How do you know when your confidence comes across as cocky, when your apathetic voice comes across as lack of confidence and when your body language is completely missing?

- How do you know where to improve and how and to what extent?

- How can you leave your comfort zone and adopt new communications pattern?

- How do you know that you are authentic or if you sound fake?

Unless you have a sparring partner to see you, feel you, hear you, you will have a hard time improving. Without a sparring partner, you might improve; but the question is how long will it take?

WHAT THE SPARRING PARTNER DOES FOR YOU

Who Can Be Your Sparring Partner?

Anybody can be a sparring partner: professionals such as peers, superiors, staff, subject-matter-experts, etc. People often make the mistake thinking that the sparring partner needs to be a professional. Your wife, your kids or grandparents can do as well. Especially when you are preparing for a complicated interview topic. You will benefit from keeping things simple. Likewise, the way to keep things simple is by talking to people who are miles away from your field of expertise and from different generations. Young kids or grandparents will do a great job in that respect. The acid test is as follows: If a six-year-old or seventy-plus grandparent understands your message, you are there.

Especially those who appear too mechanical, or too cerebral in their interviewing, will find "the naked truth" in naïve feedback from young children or grandparents. This feedback is very valuable because it helps you become more natural in the way you present yourself when talking.

Coach as Sparring Partner

To reach maximum potential, you need a coach. A coach can take you out of your comfort zone and stretch you beyond your limits to reach your full potential.

The limitations of amateurs is that good is not good enough. A professional knows what it takes to take you to peak performance in a short period of time.

BECOME AN AUTHENTIC LEADER

The toughest part of interviewing is to become authentic. And there, I see most amateur sparring partners being more confusing than helpful.

STOP SELLING

Part of being authentic is to stop the "sales talk modus operandi." It means executives are in a permanent setting of selling themselves.

Selling is poor interviewing. Nobody likes to be sold to. Interviewers smell it against the wind and want to know the other side of the coin.

The way to authentic communication is to be at peace with who you are and stop attempts at making yourself stronger than you really are or trying to appeal to the other side that you are the perfect candidate.

You present what you have, can do and excel at, but also mention the other side of the coin. Your weaknesses, shortcomings, where you need support, or coaching, or mentoring from peers or outside experts. In other words, authentic means the courage to bluntly admit what you are not good at.

TALK LESS

Another aspect of authentic communication is to deliver a short message. Executives talk too much. They are in a perpetual sales talk. When they talk about their strengths, most executives mention four to eight strengths, which is overwhelming to the listener. Talk less. Simple, short messages is what "clicks."

A good coach will help to calibrate yourself and help you find your true self. Instead of selling or overselling yourself, you simply state the truth with ease and serenity.

A good coach will help you communicate that imperfect, yet valuable solution provider – the authentic leader in you - to the interviewer, with a concise core message.

You know that this is the best you can do in an interview. The inner glow, deep satisfaction, and connectedness with your innermost self makes your interview more robust and more impactful than other rhetoric techniques. Being human and natural sells. And, it sells much better than superficial sales talk.

In this sense, the coach helps you to reach your maximum potential by becoming the most valuable version of yourself, which is the authentic leader.

FREQUENT INTERVIEWING MISTAKES AND WHAT TO DO ABOUT THEM

Mistake 1 – Memorizing scripts

Some executives try to memorize answers to the 3 PPI questions. Scripting and memorizing scripts make you weak; abandon and abstain from it. Keywords are the key, not scripts.

During your PPI Prep, apply and abide by Rapid Prototyping. Apply keywords to your interview prep. Applying 1 to 5 keywords is enough to give an outstanding outcome. Do that, and you are ready to go.

Mistake 2

Question: Who are you?

Mistake: Neglecting or ignoring the interviewer (What's in for him?) because you think and talk with a "What's in for me?" perspective.

Here's a little secret. The interviewer is obsessed with finding out as soon as possible the reason for hiring you, and that means he wants to know whether you offer superior value.

Therefore, first and foremost, re-read the question "Who are you?" Who you are is absolutely relevant and important to justify hiring you. Simply put: Why should we hire you?

WHY comes first, WHO comes second.

Mistake 3

Question: What are you good at?

Mistake: Most executives come up with a laundry list of what they are good at. Usually anything between three and up to ten skills. To show you one example, look at the following answer:

I am good at …

- Building, leading & developing people
- Creating new high value partnerships
- Simplifying Complexity
- Doing what's never been done
- Turning around underperforming businesses
- Execution
- Opening new markets
- Deliver stakeholder value

This executives says he is good at eight things. eight bullet points for eight skills. The interviewee gives eight different skills without making a choice which one is top, second, third, etc. You start to realize that this way of providing eight skills instead of one is overburdening and confusing the interviewer.

This is not a good way of answering. There is no focus and no simplicity here. Always remember these two PPI principles.

Before you attempt to answer this question, you must rephrase it: the real meaning of this question is "What are you good at that we need most?" Now we have focus. We know events, and we must address the hiring manager's biggest growth problem with our strengths.

Therefore, we can rephrase this question the second time and ask ourselves "What kind of strength do I have that I can offer, to best solve the root canal pain that the hiring manager is suffering from?"

The answer is usually simple. One, at the most two skills of yours, will suffice. Therefore, the best answer is to focus on one strength.

To pick up the above-mentioned example, one best possible answer could be as follows:

*"I am good at turning around
underperforming businesses."*

Mistake 4

Interviewees rely too much on job descriptions instead of researching the organization and the hiring manager. The job description is often too general, too superficial, and too skewed, from the real specific hiring needs and business problems of the hiring manager. Doing your research is hard work and it is only when peeling the onion again and again that you reach enough substantial insights.

BECOMING MASTERFUL AT EXECUTIVE INTERVIEWING

There is a famous saying which goes thus: "it is not the best candidate who gets the job, but the one with the best interviewing performance." Having this in mind, my mission is helping candidates become experts at executive interviewing in the shortest possible period.

For this reason, I invested a lot of time, energy, and research, into how to best prepare my candidates for job interviews. Furthermore, I attended more than a thousand real interviews as a silent observer. In addition, I directly obtained interview feedback from the decision-makers and learned how they assess and judge the quality and performance of my candidates.

As a result, I learned the underlying patterns that separate the wheat from the chaff. I learned the secrets of success and failure in interviewing. My insights applied not only to English, or Anglo-Saxon companies, it included German, French, Italian, Dutch, Danish, Finish, Swedish, Norway, Spanish, Russian, Chinese, Takalog, Arab, etc. and companies from the Americas, Europe, Middle-East and Asia. And let me repeat, being number two in my world is considered a failure.

Over the last 17 years, I have been optimizing the interviewing techniques that I am now, for the first time, presenting to you. I call them PPI.

Measure Performance in PPI

Performance in PPI is measured on a scale of 0 to 100%.

Excellent Performance

Candidates who achieve 90% or more in interview performance are categorized as excellent. I consider candidates with 90% or more of an interview performance score the ones that companies want to hire. Said the other way around, candidates below 90% are likely to fail in interviews and as such are rarely hired.

CLOSING THE GAP

As a job search coach and executive search consultant, my primary concern is to help candidates close the gap between their current performance and the 90% benchmark of excellence. A common belief of executives is that they don't have to worry about interviews. "It's going to be alright." "Somehow, I'm going to manage it," are what many of you think. Nothing is further from the truth. Most executives are likely to fail in interviews because of a serious performance gap.

TWO PILLARS
OF INTERVIEW
SUCCESS

To oversimplify your success in interviews depends on two things: be likable and offer superior value. To be likable, smile and show that you are a team player. But, what do you need to do to show them superior value? Again, it boils down to two things which I call the two pillars of interview success.

The first pillar is understanding the other side: foremost, the decision-maker. It is all about the research and investigations aimed at understanding the decision-makers problems in growing his team, unit, division, or company. It is also about gaining an understanding of the priorities, interests, and needs of the person who has the power to hire you.

The first pillar contributes to about 50% of your interview success score.

The second pillar is how and what you communicate to the other side. In other words, communication. Effective communication with the decision-maker is what PPI is about.

The second pillar PPI contributes to the other 50% of your interview success score.

What you need to realize is that to succeed in interviews, you must learn about the decision-maker and the hiring organization's hiring needs. It follows that interviewee with high interviewing power is those able to convincingly and authentically present their value through PPI while solving the decision-maker's growth problems.

I limit this book to explaining how to achieve maximum PPI performance. But, remember if you do not know the other side, you may get 50% in PPI, but still talk like a parrot or talk trash.

CONCLUSION

It is not the best candidate who gets the job but the one who interviews best. PPI helps you to achieve exactly that.

Instead of diluting your efforts with too many questions in mind, PPI provides radical focus on the three most important interview questions.

Then, PPI helps you to shift from overly long and random answers towards well-structured and engaging communication with the interviewer because you apply the three PPI techniques.

Finally, PPI is powerful because it is simple. Less is more. Executives who tend to talk too much become concise and to the point.

In a nutshell, applying PPI ultimately enables you to succinctly present yourself and to communicate your irresistible value to the hiring manager so that you get shortlisted as must-hire candidate.

While it takes only one hour to learn PPI, excellence in PPI requires repetition. Rehearse, and rehearse again. Only then will you reap the full benefits of the PPI methodology and get masterful at interviewing.

ENDNOTES

MORITA, Rainer, *"Executive Job Search in the Hidden Job Market – The Morita Method"*, CreateSpace Publishing, 2017

Printed in France by Amazon
Brétigny-sur-Orge, FR

16032034R00033